BUSINESS MODELS FOR IMPLEMENTING GEOSPATIAL TECHNOLOGIES IN TRANSPORTATION DECISION-MAKING

Prepared for:
Office of Interstate and Border Planning
Federal Highway Administration
U.S. Department of Transportation

Prepared by:
Planning and Policy Analysis Division
John A. Volpe National Transportation Systems Center
Research and Innovative Technology Administration
U.S. Department of Transportation

TABLE OF CONTENTS

EXECUTIVE SUMMARY 3

I. BACKGROUND 3

II. Arizona DOT Case Study: *Emergence of GIS from a need to address federal requirements* 7

III. Delaware DOT Case Study: *Unique Business Model to Support an Enterprise-wide GIS Application* 12

IV. Georgia DOT Case Study: *An Information Technology-based GIS Business Model* 15

V. Montana DOT Case Study: *Considerations for Implementing a Strategic Plan for GIS* 19

VI. North Carolina DOT Case Study *Organizing a sizeable GIS team* 22

VII. Oklahoma DOT Case Study: *Pilot demonstration to support enterprise GIS development* ... 25

VIII. COMPARISON OF CASE STUDIES 29

IX. CRITICAL SUCCESS FACTORS AND RECOMMENDATIONS 31

    Key Success Factors and Recommendations 31

    Recommendations on FHWA's Role in Supporting Geospatial Technology Implementation at State DOTs 33

APPENDIX A. PRE-INTERVIEW QUESTIONNAIRE 35

APPENDIX B. INTERVIEW GUIDE 36

LIST OF FIGURES

Figure 1: Organizational chart for the Arizona Department of Transportation

Figure 2: Organization chart For the Arizona Department of Transportation's Data Bureau.

Figure 3: Organizational chart for the Delaware Department of Transportation

Figure 4: Organizational chart for the Georgia Department of Transportation

Figure 5: Organizational chart for the Montana Department of Transportation

Figure 6: Organizational chart for the Information Technology Division of the North Carolina GIS Unit

Figure 7: Organizational chart for the Planning and Research Division of the Oklahoma Department of Transportation

EXECUTIVE SUMMARY

For several decades, many government agencies and other organizations have used geospatial technologies to input, store, retrieve, manipulate, analyze, and output geographically referenced (location-based), or "geospatial," data. With Geographic Information Systems (GIS) to organize these data, users can easily:

- Store and query complex information about locations' various attributes.
- Make consistent maps for visualization and/or analysis.
- Communicate information.
- Make better decisions.

At State Departments of Transportation (DOTs), where nearly all transportation decisions are in some way tied to geography, geospatial technologies are becoming increasingly advanced and useful tools. These technologies are helping State DOTs to more cost-effectively and efficiently deliver needed transportation improvements to the public.

While some State DOTs use stand-alone applications to serve specific, individual business needs, others have developed or are developing enterprise solutions that address a range of business requirements across the organization. In both cases, factors such as early history, data development and management arrangements, funding availability, and organizational structure shape State DOTs' abilities to apply geospatial data to improve decision-making.

This report describes six State DOTs' business models for implementing geospatial technologies. It provides a comparison of the organizational factors influencing how Arizona DOT, Delaware DOT, Georgia DOT, Montana DOT, North Carolina DOT, and Oklahoma DOT invest in and use geospatial information to support their respective business needs. Critical success factors identified by each DOT are also documented, along with suggestions for how the Federal Highway Administration (FHWA) might better support State DOTs in implementing geospatial programs.

In general, at State DOTs the early history of implementing GIS and data development considerations have been significant contributors to determining how GIS activities are arranged organizationally. Some GIS programs originated in response to a need for providing maps more quickly. Others developed applications to meet specific business needs that had been communicated from various divisions across the organization.

State DOTs have obtained data in a variety of ways, including developing their own data from digitizing paper maps or purchasing commercially available data. In all cases, the interviewed State DOTs have developed or are moving toward creating an enterprise GIS. Such systems enable access to information across multiple divisions regardless of familiarity with GIS, allowing greater efficiency, public transparency, and quicker and better decision-making.

Key activities for successful implementation of geospatial technologies identified during interviews include:

- Develop upper-level management support and maintain strong relationships.
- Poll staff and assess business requirements.
- Create a permanent GIS Steering Committee.
- Appoint/designate a permanent GIS coordinator.
- Work to build fast applications.
- Select and define the data architecture for the GIS environment.
- Seek to secure funding for GIS projects from multiple partners, both internally and externally.

- Evaluate available GIS software solutions and document a selected standard.
- Evaluate implemented GIS solutions and document a selected standard.
- Work closely with FHWA.
- Never give up the dream.

These factors are described in more detail in Section IX. Critical Success Factors and Recommendations.

I. BACKGROUND

Between November 2005 and February 2006, the Federal Highway Administration (FHWA) Office of Interstate and Border Planning (HEPI) conducted a domestic scan with transportation executives to identify critical information that decision-makers need to make informed decisions and investments in the latest geospatial technologies. During the scan, the state of the art in the use of geospatial technology for transportation at state and local levels was explored and practices for successful implementation were shared. Afterward, FHWA HEPI and the Transportation Research Board (TRB) hosted a one-day workshop to discuss these and other findings.

The goal of the workshop, which had the participation of transportation executives from across the nation, was to draft an action plan that would help to guide FHWA, state DOTs, and other transportation partners in their efforts to best apply geospatial technologies to future transportation decision-making.[1] One of the recommended actions stemming from the workshop was to document business models that state DOTs are using to implement geospatial technologies for improved transportation decision-making. This action would help to diffuse the effective business practices of selected state DOTs to others that may not have had the experience or success of their counterparts.

As a first step toward learning and disseminating these experiences and lessons learned, the USDOT Volpe National Transportation Systems Center (Volpe Center), in coordination with FHWA HEPI, worked to identify a list of state DOTs with noteworthy business practices for implementing geospatial technologies.[2] The Volpe Center then conducted a series of interviews with a GIS manager or higher-level staff in each of the following six state DOTs:

- Arizona DOT
- Delaware DOT
- Georgia DOT
- Montana DOT
- North Carolina DOT
- Oklahoma DOT

Conversations with these DOTs were steered by a Pre-interview Questionnaire and an Interview Guide (see Appendices A and B). Each case study includes a discussion of the DOT's early history with geospatial technologies, the business model for implementing the technologies, and activities that the state views as critical for securing lasting endorsement of geospatial technologies. In conclusion, a summary comparing implementation insights and recommendations among the six case studies is offered, as well as suggestions for how FHWA might better support state DOTs in implementing geospatial programs.

- **Case Study 1** explores how GIS, initially emerging in Arizona DOT from a need to comply with federal requirements, has gained strength at the Department.

- **Case Study 2** examines Delaware DOT's enterprise-wide GIS application and the unique organizational structure that supports it.

---

[1] To see the complete Executive Scan Tour report, visit www.gis.fhwa.dot.gov/execscan.asp.
[2] A preliminary list of potential State DOTs to interview was generated through reviewing notes collected during the domestic scan and GIS-T presentations archived online at www.gis-t.org/. This list was narrowed to six to include State DOTs of varying size, geographic location, and demonstrated GIS success. The State DOTs included in this report do not represent a complete list of State DOTs with effective business models and practices in implementing geospatial technology activities.

- **Case Study 3** considers Georgia DOT's information technology (IT)-based business model for implementing GIS.

- **Case Study 4** describes Montana DOT's effort to develop a strategic plan for implementing GIS, and the special considerations that were involved.

- **Case Study 5** discusses how North Carolina DOT has organized its GIS Unit, which has over 50 full-time employees, to provide for active contributions to the statewide GIS community.

- **Case Study 6** focuses on how a pilot demonstration helped Oklahoma DOT to develop an enterprise GIS.

II. ARIZONA DOT CASE STUDY:
Emergence of GIS from a Need to Address Federal Requirements

CONTACT: JAMI RAE GARRISON, (602) 712-8958
E-MAIL: JGarrison@azdot.gov

Background

Arizona's Department of Transportation (ADOT) first began using systems that would eventually evolve into Geographic Information Systems (GIS) in the early 1970s. Early on, ADOT used a graphical mainframe application as part of its efforts to comply with the National Highway Safety Act of 1966,[3] which established the first requirements for statewide traffic records systems. The Act subsequently detailed terms for the recording and reporting of accidents on and off the State Highway System. In response, ADOT used proprietary software to develop the Accident Location Information Surveillance System (ALISS), which contained crash data and associated spatial information.

In 1993 and 1994, a conversion process was initiated to make the spatial data housed in ALISS part of a "modern" GIS. Since then, GIS has gained strength throughout ADOT for its usefulness as a technology tool in planning, analyzing, modeling, and managing both spatial and tabular information. Now, the data originally part of ALISS comprise a base-layer coverage of Arizona's roads and streets, known as the Arizona Transportation Information System (ATIS), or ATIS Roads. This application, which is continually being developed and improved, is discussed in detail below.

Business Model for Geospatial Technology Implementation

Organizational Structure and Funding

During the early stages of GIS development at ADOT, detailed crash data housed in ALISS were collected and maintained in the Department's Traffic Records Group. As ADOT began to convert the ALISS data into a more modern GIS, a team comprising members from its Transportation Planning Division, Information Technology Section, and Photogrammetry/Survey Section was formed to better manage the spatial data. Using ESRI's ArcInfo software, ADOT worked to migrate ALISS's spatial data into a full GIS database as the centerline data for the State Highway System. When this activity was completed, data maintenance was assigned to the Transportation Planning Division.

A GIS-Transportation (GIS-T) Section, which is organizationally located within the Data Bureau of the Transportation Planning Division (Figure 1), coordinates the Department's GIS activities, including maintenance of the ATIS Roads GIS database.

---

[3] National Highway Safety Act: http://nhtsa.gov/nhtsa/Cfc_title49/HighwaySafety.html#402.

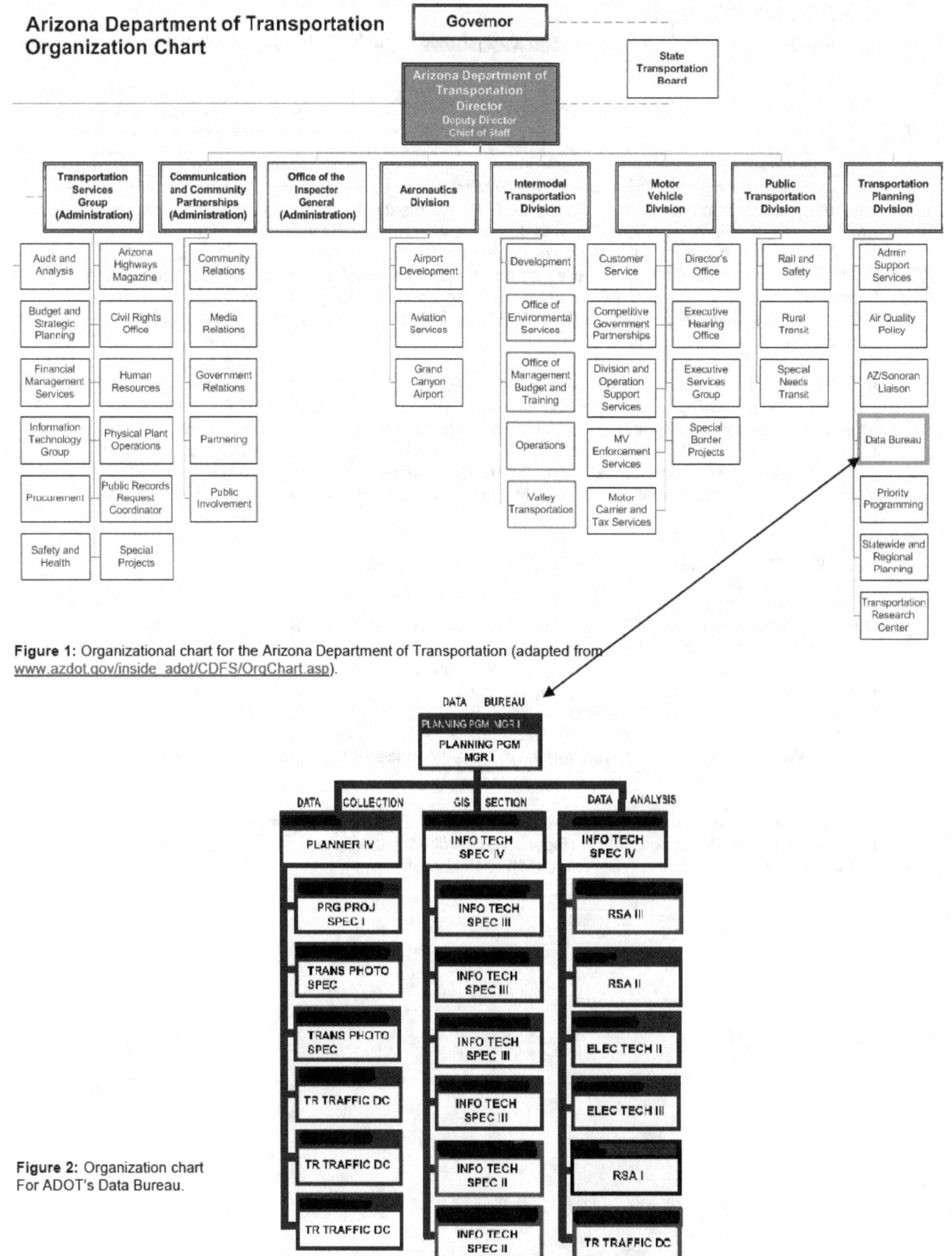

Figure 1: Organizational chart for the Arizona Department of Transportation (adapted from www.azdot.gov/inside_adot/CDFS/OrgChart.asp).

Figure 2: Organization chart For ADOT's Data Bureau.

Funding comes primarily from FHWA's State Planning and Research (SPR) program. Each year, the manager of the Data Bureau develops a budget, which is reviewed and approved by the director of the Transportation Planning Division and the FHWA Division Office. In the future, there may be opportunities for certain projects or applications to be funded by other sources.

The GIS-T Section's annual budget for project work and GIS maintenance is approximately $500,000. However, in some years the budget is due more to significant one-time project costs.

ADOT's GIS-T section employs seven full-time staff, one of whom is the manager. In the past, staff turnover has been high, with many employees leaving for higher-paying jobs with local agencies or the private sector. Currently, however, the section has reached nearly full staffing levels. While state funding helps to support these labor costs, there is no DOT-wide or statewide GIS software purchase program. This means that groups using geospatial technologies within each Arizona agency must draw from their respective budgets to buy their own software from vendors as needed.

The use of SPR funds requires quarterly reports to FHWA, which include status, accomplishments, and setbacks for all ongoing projects. This information is summarized on an annual basis and presented along with the budget request. Additional oversight is provided by the state's Government Information Technology Agency (GITA), which reviews any project involving information technology resources with a budget of more than $25,000.

Roles and Responsibilities
ADOT's GIS-T Section collects, maintains, and distributes geospatial data. Some data, such as those about bridges and incidents, are supplied to the GIS-T Section from other groups within ADOT. On occasion, consultants have been used for data creation, but maintenance responsibilities have always been given to ADOT.

Data are made available freely for noncommercial use, although some data may require the user to have ESRI software. For all data sharing, ADOT requires that requestors, including other government agencies at the state or local level, complete data release forms. Certain data, such as crash data, cannot be made available unless it is first cleaned of sensitive personal information. Since this process can be time-consuming, current data are not always available for immediate distribution. ADOT's Risk Management Office evaluates and handles requests for use by commercial entities or for any type of legal use.

Programs and Services
To distribute geospatial data, ADOT's primary application is the Arizona Transportation Information System (ATIS), otherwise known as ATIS Roads. The ATIS Roads database contains information on centerlines and mile markers for the entire Arizona State Highway System, including ramps and frontage roads, with annual maintenance performed in-house using GPS. Data are also kept on local road centerlines, and ADOT receives this information directly from local municipalities as available. ADOT releases quarterly updates of its centerline data, which have been used to build a linear referencing system.

ADOT also provides the following notable services:

- *Internet Map Server*[4]—The Internet Map Server is a tool that allows various stakeholders to view ADOT data. ADOT intends to deploy an enhanced sever in the near future to provide greater access to data. Certain data are not available to the public on this server but are served internally by a data warehouse.

---

[4] ADOT's Internet Map Server: http://tpd.azdot.gov/website/.

- *PhotoLog Data Viewer*—The PhotoLog Data Viewer offers a video record of the entire Arizona State Highway System. Sites for viewing can be selected via route/milepost and offset for any location across the state. The video made available on the PhotoLog is captured annually as staff drive the system collecting GPS centerlines, crossing features, and mile-marker locations. The PhotoLog is available internally at ADOT and externally for noncommercial use by special arrangement.

- *ADOT Map Book*[5]—The ADOT Map Book is a collection of maps most often requested and used within ADOT as well as maps that represent multimodal aspects of the agency.

- *GIS-T Section Team*—The GIS-T Section Team is committed to providing support to ADOT for the many projects that contain a GIS component. Some support areas include:
    - The Crash Database
    - Highway Performance Monitoring System (HPMS)
    - Az511—real-time traffic data and closures/restrictions[6]
    - State Highway Log
    - Five-Year Construction Program
    - Arizona Information Data Warehouse (AIDW)
    - Oversize/overweight truck permitting
    - Storm water management
    - Environmental planning studies

Obstacles

Limitations in acquiring spatial road data from some local agencies have posed a significant challenge. These agencies' ability to produce and package spatial data is limited by their small size and limited budget or technical capabilities. Much of Arizona is rural, and many smaller cities and counties do not have dedicated full-time or part-time GIS staffs. Although local agencies may be able to afford the expense of purchasing GIS software, often they cannot afford to hire the staff needed to maintain a GIS infrastructure. Additionally, a significant portion of Arizona is tribal land. Each tribe managing this land is unique, and establishing spatial data-sharing arrangements with the tribes often requires a complex, variable process. Some Native American nations are concerned that the implications of sharing road data with Arizona DOT might include an increase in non-local traffic, as not all tribal roads are in a condition to receive higher traffic volumes.

One possible way of helping local agencies in their role as data providers is to use funding that the agencies have received from the state's E911 program to build local road databases. It is hoped that any data created as part of this program could be shared with ADOT. Agreements for sharing the data, and standards for data quality and formatting, are still being discussed; ADOT is unable to impose standards for data that it receives, but the Department can issue guidelines and promote their benefits.

Arizona's GIS Community

Arizona's state government has a very cooperative GIS community. One forum for this coordination is the Arizona Geographic Information Council (AGIC).[7] AGIC comprises governor-appointed executive members as well as other representatives from state agencies, large universities, federal groups such as the U.S. Geological Survey (USGS), and tribal governments. AGIC and the State Cartographer's Office[8] have worked together to set up a clearinghouse to store and redistribute GIS data. ADOT plays a prominent role in AGIC, having developed expertise through working with spatial data for many years. The governor-appointed ADOT

---

[5] ADOT Map Book: http://tpd.azdot.gov/gis/maps/pdf/Section_One.pdf.
[6] ADOT's 511: www.az511.com.
[7] AGIC website: http://agic.az.gov/.
[8] State Cartographer Office website: http://sco.az.gov/.

representative to the AGIC executive board served as vice president in 2001–2002 and as president in 2002–2003. ADOT has assisted AGIC in the acquisition of updated DOQQ imagery for the state and actively serves on several committees, including planning for the annual AGIC conference, the Homeland Security Committee, and a Transportation Working Group.

AGIC is funded by contributions from all of the participating agencies, which pay varying amounts on the basis of their size and funding levels. Its projects benefit the entire state GIS community. For instance, AGIC coordinated with the U.S. Geological Survey to update the digital imagery for Arizona.

A GIS Steering Committee is also being convened within ADOT, with the first meeting scheduled for February 2007. ADOT anticipates that policy decisions for ADOT GIS will go through this committee as an advisory board to the GIS-T Section Team.

III. DELAWARE CASE STUDY:
Unique Business Model to Support an Enterprise-wide GIS Application

CONTACT: MATTHEW LAICK, (302) 760-2661
E-MAIL: MATTHEW.LAICK@STATE.DE.US

Background

The implementation of geospatial technologies at Delaware DOT (DelDOT) has matured in response to a need for an efficient and cost-effective means of tracking transportation assets in Delaware. Since the early stages of developing the first geospatial applications at DelDOT, support for the use of geospatial data has been strong and apparent at all levels of the organization. Although the benefits of geospatial technologies have not been formally measured, an intuitive understanding of its usefulness has pervaded DelDOT business. Enthusiastic, purposeful champions from mid-level management have historically been able to communicate to others within the Department how geospatial data underlies a majority of the DOT's decisions.

The widespread support for using geospatial technologies for improved decision-making recently helped to enable DelDOT to develop and deploy a comprehensive, user-friendly, enterprise-wide GIS. Since its initial release in 2004, DelDOT's Information Network for Online Resource Mapping (INFORM) system has become the primary tool for mapping and viewing geospatial data within the Department. With INFORM, all staff can access geospatial data efficiently on their own desktops without needing additional software or training. The tool and how it supports DelDOT's unique business model is discussed in more detail below.

Business Model for Geospatial Technology Implementation

Geospatial activities at DelDOT, which are primarily funded by a capital budget, are spread throughout the entire organization. The Technology and Support Services Division is responsible for building DelDOT's geospatial applications, but several divisions within the Department have GIS specialists on staff and perform geospatial work (Figure 3). For example, both the Technology and Support Services Division and the Planning Division employ three GIS specialists, while several others are on staff in DOT divisions such as Transportation Assets and Engineering Systems. To varying degrees, most staff within the Department have become capable GIS users with the deployment of INFORM.

Although geospatial activities are distributed across divisional boundaries, divisions have worked to maintain close and fluid coordination. There is continued discussion among the various divisions' GIS specialists. This interaction is informal but steady and often offers opportunity for on-the-job training. The divisions have also worked to craft very specific job descriptions for GIS specialists, helping to ensure that skills are matched appropriately with divisions' business needs.

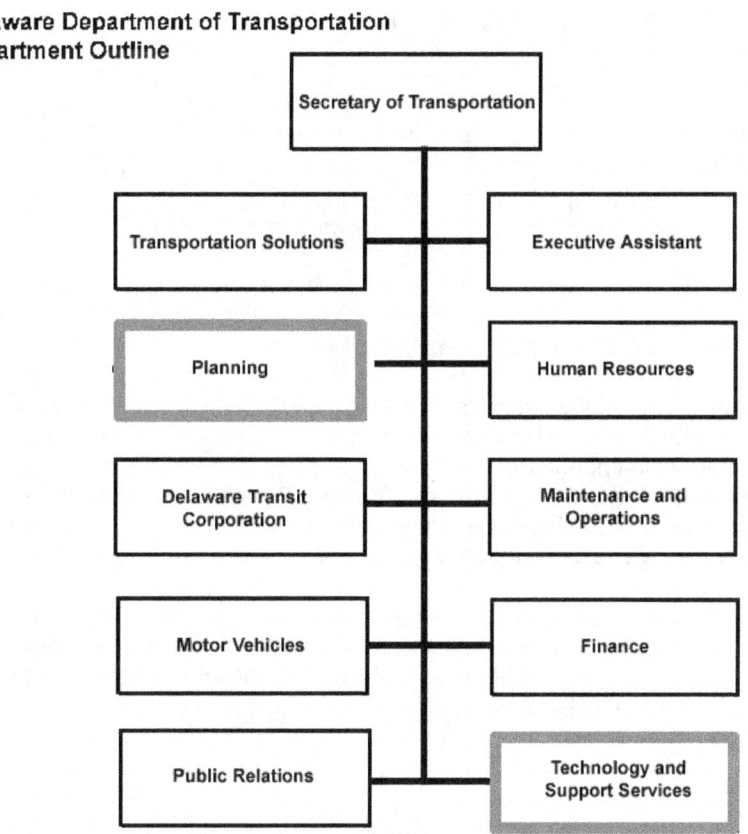

Figure 3: Organizational chart for the Delaware Department of Transportation (adapted from organizational chart at www.deldot.gov/static/org_chart-2006e.pdf).

External Data-Sharing Opportunities
There is widespread cooperation for sharing geospatial data in Delaware. DelDOT both shares and obtains geospatial data with counterpart agencies with relative ease. This relationship is in part due to the evolution of Delaware's Data Mapping and Integration Library (DataMIL).[9] Originally a pilot project for the USGS National Map, Delaware DataMIL, which provides an Internet Mapping Service for the State of Delaware, serves Delaware's Spatial Data Framework, or basic map datasets. State agencies, local and county governments, academic GIS users, and the private sector can build their own GIS data on the Framework. These datasets are considered the most current and up-to-date base map information available for Delaware; a data steward is identified to take ownership of each dataset and to publish the only "official" dataset for that part of the Framework. Datasets that change frequently are updated at least quarterly.

Information Network for Online Resource Mapping (INFORM)
DelDOT's INFORM application is a GIS-enabled intranet portal that provides DelDOT employees with enterprise transportation data using a quick, efficient, and user-friendly interface. The system allows users with all levels of GIS expertise to quickly search, access, visualize, and analyze geospatial data essential for Delaware's transportation operations. As GeoDecisions, developer of the application, has explained, INFORM:

---

[9] See Delaware's DataMIL at http://datamil.delaware.gov/ and the Delaware Geospatial Information Clearinghouse at http://maps.rdms.udel.edu/Portal/.

- Provides access to transportation data through a web-enabled GIS portal.
- Interfaces with asset management systems.
- Eliminates data redundancy and provides a single source for enterprise information.
- Allows data to be kept up to date by "business owners," or those responsible for managing the respective datasets; for example, the roadway network is managed by the Technology and Support Services Division, which can enter and change the data.
- Provides data input and data editing capabilities.
- Provides a comprehensive base network for all public roads.

One of the most unique aspects of INFORM is that DelDOT's geospatial data are now found at one centralized location. This helps to eliminate data redundancy, providing the ability to meet many business needs with a single geospatial database.

Prior to this application, data were maintained in several locations, requiring DelDOT employees to have GIS software on their desktops to access spatial data and create maps. Now, all INFORM users have the ability to change data in the business applications they manage (e.g. the road inventory by the Planning Division). Any modifications that INFORM users make are immediately reflected as updates to the entire database. This ensures that everyone at DelDOT is working with the most accurate and current data.

With the INFORM application, DelDOT requires less GIS software—a significant cost savings to the Department. DelDOT GIS specialists can also now focus on data and applications development and maintenance rather than on having to address individual requests for maps, training, and other geospatial needs.

IV. GEORGIA CASE STUDY:
An Information Technology-based GIS Business Model

CONTACT: TEAGUE BUCHANAN, ENTERPRISE GIS MANAGER, (404) 463-2860 X137
E-MAIL: TEAGUE.BUCHANAN@DOT.STATE.GA.US

Background

Georgia DOT (GDOT) first used GIS in the early 1990s, when it released the Georgia Navigator System, an ITS (Intelligent Transportation System) application. This system, which contained components of ESRI's ArcInfo software and used a purchased spatial dataset, helped state government personnel to locate traffic incidents, view them in context, and efficiently plan and communicate alternate routes. Once in place, the utility of the Georgia Navigator quickly became widely apparent. GDOT studies indicated that, for every traffic accident Georgia Navigator helped to clear efficiently, 14 additional accidents were prevented. Given this success rate and the timing of the system's development and implementation (it was in place and working in advance of the 1996 Olympic Games in Atlanta), a strong case was made for GIS implementation to improve decision-making in the state.

Shortly after deployment of the Georgia Navigator System, GDOT decided to begin developing its own spatial data. Since GDOT is responsible for tracking and mapping all public roads in Georgia, the manual updating of general highway maps—a task performed by the Department from 1960 to 1992—was extremely time-consuming. In 1992, GDOT formed a contractual partnership with the Information Technology Outreach Services (ITOS) Center of the University of Georgia's Carl Vinson Institute of Government to digitize all road data contained in GDOT's map sheets. The partnership also worked to digitize linear referencing attributes from GDOT's roadway characteristics (RC) inventory database. University students performed much of the digitizing work, providing them with hands-on GIS experience and delivering cost savings to GDOT.

Since then, GDOT has worked to overcome a variety of challenges, such as:

- Data-quality and scaling issues caused by layering digitized roads data (1:31,680 scale) on digital orthophotography quarter quadrangles (1:12,000 scale).
- Occasional funding issues.
- The need to reconcile the RC inventory database with sophisticated spatial data.
- Uneven access to spatial data resources by GDOT staff due to variable GIS expertise across the Department.

GDOT is working to continue improving the ways that it maintains, shares, and displays geospatial data as well as to create applications accessible to users throughout the agency and to the public.

Business Model for Geospatial Technology Implementation

In 2000, personnel from many divisions across GDOT who had a certain level of computer skills were brought together to form the Division of Information Technology (IT) (Figure 4).

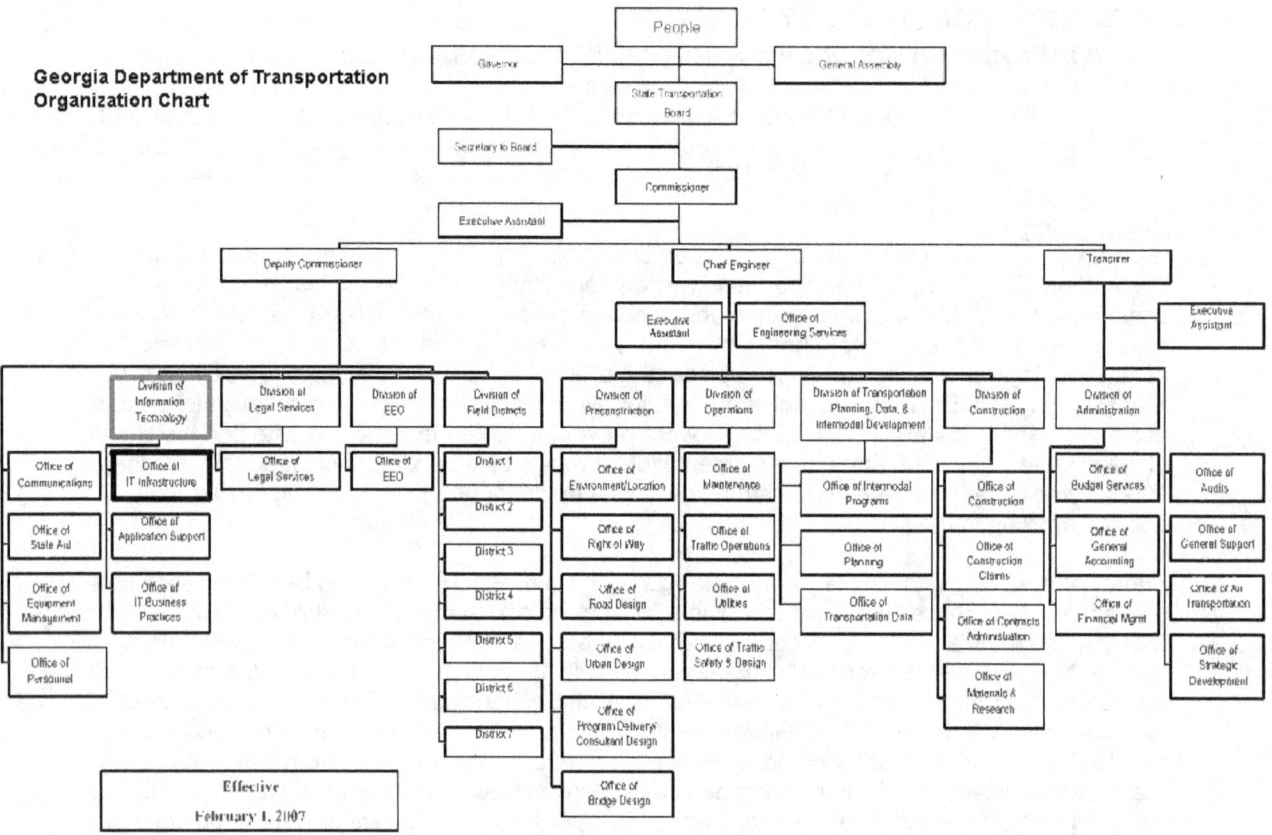

Figure 4: Organizational chart for the Georgia Department of Transportation (adapted from www.dot.state.ga.us/documents/pdf/orgchart/gdot-orgchart.pdf).

By 2003, the Division had reached an organizational maturity level at which it was able to provide the expertise required to maintain and grow GDOT's spatial data infrastructure as well as to support customers throughout GDOT, including engineering, planning, and environmental staff. Currently, there are approximately 150 people in the IT Division, 24 of whom work with GIS.

Funding and Data Maintenance
The annual budget for GIS at GDOT is approximately $1.8 million, most of which comes out of State Planning and Research (SPR) funds. A steering team has been formed to assist the IT Division in deciding how to allocate its budget across projects. Although GDOT's two largest GIS costs are labor and hardware, software is also a significant expense; the Department is the largest government customer in Georgia of ESRI GIS software. Interagency negotiations are currently ongoing to arrange an enterprise-wide GIS software licensing agreement through the Georgia Technology Authority (GTA), a statutorily established entity. Georgia will collaboratively develop a set of commonly used statewide GIS databases needed by multiple agencies.

Agencies that purchase ESRI software through the GTA licensing program must agree to provide their data to the Georgia Spatial Data Infrastructure (GSDI).[10] The GSDI was formed to allow state agencies to collaboratively develop a set of commonly used statewide GIS databases needed by multiple agencies. The GSDI is home to a GIS Data Clearinghouse, a shared effort between the University of Georgia and Georgia Institute of Technology to make the application of spatial information technologies more efficient by eliminating duplication in the production and

---

[10] Georgia Spatial Data Infrastructure: www.gis.state.ga.us.

distribution of spatial data. It is expected that the GIS Data Clearinghouse will help agencies with limited funding or staff resources to develop and maintain their GIS infrastructures. Similarly, since GDOT maintains only transportation spatial data and cannot afford to maintain all data layers for the state, it is dependent on other agencies for information such as boundaries and hydrology data. The GIS Data Clearinghouse is a significant resource for GDOT.

At the state level, GDOT plays an active role in the GIS Coordinating Committee, which consists of representatives from various interested state agencies and the private sector. Participation is on an ad hoc, voluntary basis. The GIS Coordinating Committee provides a forum for raising a greater awareness of statewide GIS needs within its members.

According to GDOT, cost recovery has not been a viable option for GIS at a statewide level since data on this scale are often more generalized than are local data. It is possible that the selling of data products might be more feasible for city and county organizations that have created localized data containing high levels of detail. The real return on investment for GDOT has been realized through information sharing with state-agency counterparts and through being able to offer staff and the public firsthand access to data.

GDOT's Transportation Explorer (TREX)

For many years, uneven GIS expertise prevented a majority of GDOT staff from accessing the Department's GIS data and resources, and it became apparent that GIS knowledge could not be a prerequisite for the wide diversity of customers that could benefit from GIS. In response, GDOT developed the Transportation Explorer (TREX), now the Department's most prominent GIS application. TREX is a web portal system that serves as both an internal GIS information clearinghouse (85 available layers) and an application that allows the public real-time access to GDOT maps, reports, plans, videologs, and ITS cameras for the entire state (23 available layers). In 2005, TREX received the Georgia Technology Conference Best of Georgia Award for Redefining Government and was runner-up for the URISA Exemplary Systems in Government Award.

Recently, the TREX architecture was redesigned to better support non-GIS users' ability to create, modify, and print maps. GDOT engaged ESRI professional services to assist with the technical aspects of the redesign. GDOT technology developers were trained to create and support applications under a new technology framework.[11] As a result, Georgia DOT believes it has better defined an applications development framework to incorporate GIS into IT applications.

Enterprise GIS Needs Assessment

In 2005, GDOT conducted an enterprise GIS needs assessment, which documented the Department's internal baseline needs for GIS. Seven enterprise GIS program initiatives were identified as priorities:

1. **Mapping on Demand**—Provide non-GIS users with the ability to create, modify, and print user-defined maps in multiple formats.
2. **CAD Interoperability**—Provide data interoperability between MicroStation and ArcGIS, allowing access to CAD datasets for GIS data mapping, data mining, and analysis.
3. **Asset Location**—Provide centralized GIS datasets that allow identification and location of GDOT transportation structures, facilities, and equipment.
4. **Data Analysis**—Provide end-user/end-provider interfaces and applications to support analysis of environmental, safety, traffic, intermodal connectivity, project planning/location, and economic data.
5. **Work Activity Tracking**—Provide real-time tracking applications that monitor the status and retain the history of work being performed by mobile field workers.

---

[11] ESRI assisted GDOT in redesigning TREX's framework to function with ESRI's ArcGIS 9.2 Java Application Development Framework for ArcIMS and ArcGIS Server.

6. **Open Data Exchange**—Provide data transformation, metadata, and data delivery services that will facilitate the free and open exchange of spatial data within and among GDOT and its transportation partners.
7. **Building the GDOT GIS**—Provide the GIS framework to support the collection, maintenance, security, accessibility, performance, replication, and versioning of GIS data. This framework includes enterprise GIS architecture and services.

IT development activities and resources have been aligned to begin the implementation of projects to deliver these capabilities. Mapping on Demand, CAD Interoperability, and Building the GDOT GIS were selected as the first three initiatives in which projects would be implemented.

In 2006, GDOT documented its existing GIS architecture and identified needs and gaps in developing an enterprise GIS. The resulting recommendations, which served as a valuable communications tool with IT staff and contractors, formed a basis for aligning an enterprise GIS architecture as effectively as possible with the business needs of the Department. Now, GDOT has defined, and continues to refine, a framework to support an enterprise GIS. Later in 2007, GDOT anticipates pursuing activities to improve the stability of the enterprise GIS. In addition, an enterprise GIS Strategic Plan is being developed to better communicate to decision-makers how the enterprise GIS program will be delivered to fulfill the business needs of GDOT.

GDOT is currently evaluating the subsidization of high-quality GPS units for use within the agency and the provision of a support framework for those units. Some of the current local data collection is performed with inexpensive, imprecise equipment. If better equipment were available, data quality could be improved to the point where it could be shared more easily across the entire organization.

V. MONTANA CASE STUDY:
Considerations for Implementing a Strategic Plan for GIS

CONTACT: BILL CLOUD, (406) 444-6114
MARLIN SANDER, (406) 444-9294
E-MAIL: bcloud@mt.gov
msander@mt.gov

Background

The Montana Department of Transportation (MDT) first used geospatial technologies in 1994. Early on, there were little or no set criteria for gauging business needs within MDT's various divisions. For this reason, the Department's geospatial activities were primarily application-based; applications that were developed were often built in a somewhat ad hoc manner on the basis of perceived requirements of MDT division staff. Over time, it became apparent that these applications might not be in alignment with specific business needs.

Now, MDT is making a focused effort to develop a geospatial infrastructure and plan for a program that answers the question, "What do we need?" In doing so, MDT is establishing a more efficient, cost-effective, and user-friendly means for managing, maintaining, and monitoring the geospatial data underlying its business activities and decisions.

In January 2007, MDT released its GIS Strategic Plan. The Plan, produced by a consultant, sets forth a deliberate course of action for maximizing resources devoted to the management and maintenance of geospatial data. It provides a strategic direction for GIS investment while improving workflow in and among divisions. The Plan also examines how geospatial data and applications can be incorporated into planned and existing management systems, support new integrated initiatives, promote enterprise data management, and make information more accessible within MDT for better decision-making. The cost of fully implementing the GIS Strategic Plan is estimated to be $9 million if the majority of the work is outsourced.

Business Model for Geospatial Technology Implementation

GIS activities at MDT are managed by two divisions: the Rail, Transit and Planning Division and the Information Services Division (ISD) (Figure 5).

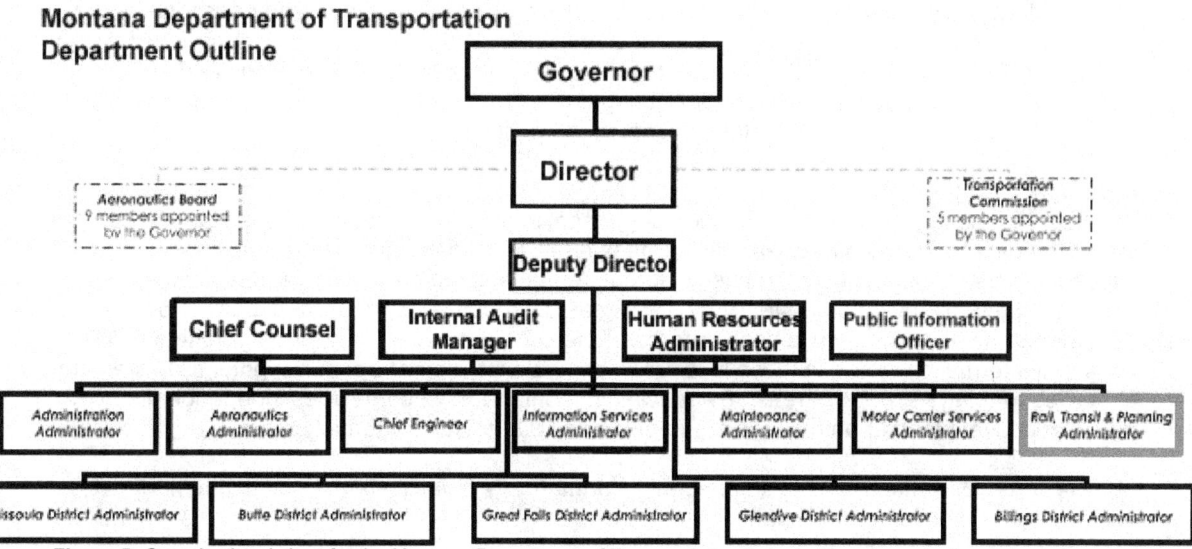

Figure 5: Organizational chart for the Montana Department of Transportation (adapted from organizational chart at www.mdt.mt.gov/mdt/contacts.shtml).

The Rail, Transit and Planning Division, which comprises the Data and Statistics Bureau, the Multimodal Planning Bureau, the Project Analysis Bureau, and the Program and Policy Analysis Bureau, provides a broad range of multimodal planning, program, and data collection and analysis functions. The Data and Statistics Bureau is responsible for collecting, processing, analyzing, and reporting general transportation infrastructure data for the state; it also performs a majority of the Department's statewide mapping activities and geospatial data distribution. Within the Data and Statistics Bureau, five staff positions are dedicated to GIS, three of which are GIS specialists.

The ISD also plays a role in the implementation of MDT's geospatial technology activities. The Division, which delivers IT support to MDT, develops a majority of the geospatial data standards for the Department. ISD also builds the geospatial applications that are ultimately used by the Rail, Transit and Planning Division and others.

While the ISD and the Rail, Transit, and Planning Division perform different work functions, the offices work together very closely. ISD performs infrastructure, spatial data management, applications development, training, security, and storage functions as well as the traditional GIS data integration. The Rail, Transit, and Planning Division performs infrastructure data collection, road log management, and mapping functions.

To enhance coordination regarding geospatial activities between these and other divisions within MDT, a GIS Steering Committee consisting of mid-level managers was developed. The committee first worked to help interpret MDT's business requirements (developed by an independent contractor through interviews with over 480 personnel) for incorporation in the GIS Strategic Plan. The committee initially met once a week, but later, as the project developed, it convened whenever its input was needed.

Historically, MDT has always had an executive-level advocate for GIS, and the GIS Steering Committee has helped to strengthen awareness among MDT executives as to how geospatial data can facilitate improved decision-making. Similarly, an IT board convenes at the state level to provide a forum to guide state agencies in the development, deployment, and advancement of intergovernmental IT resources. Established by Senate Bill 131, the board consists of all division and deputy administrators from Montana's state agencies. Board meetings are held in order to:

- Make counterpart agencies aware of what is going on within the IT and geospatial realm at each agency.
- Advise the Department of Administration (DOA) on statewide IT standards and policies, the state strategic IT plan, major IT budget requests, and rates charged for services.
- Establish priorities for the state's geospatial activities.

Data Consistency
At times, the management and distribution of geospatial data in Montana has been somewhat of a free-for-all. The DOA works to ensure that the state's IT infrastructure is reliable, secure, and cost-effective and that it meets the business requirements of state agencies and residents. It has also attempted to provide consistency by serving as a geospatial data clearinghouse. However, data standards have not always been enforced. The DOA manages three GIS layers that MDT uses, but information stored in these layers can originate from other agencies, potentially creating obstacles to analysis. For this reason, agencies in Montana have sometimes independently developed layers that, upon request, are supplied to MDT to store internally.

MDT is currently working with its state-agency counterparts to facilitate the development of data, security, and management standards.

Obstacles
Both the Rail, Transit and Planning Division and the ISD have faced challenges in bringing geospatial technologies into prevalence at MDT. The Rail, Transit and Planning Division is not organizationally structured in a way that makes it possible to know whether its efforts are being duplicated elsewhere in MDT. Thus, there has been a need, which is now being addressed through the GIS Strategic Plan, to cooperate and explicitly define who will be doing which activities.

The ISD has sometimes had issues with the funding of geospatial activities. Many of the ISD's projects are not as high-profile as those of the Rail, Transit and Planning Division; thus, little or no return-on-investment or cost-benefit analyses have been conducted. The GIS Strategic Plan will seek to address this deficit by including measures for assessing the costs and benefits of GIS applications across divisional boundaries.

Additionally, the ISD is tasked with responding to the varying needs of MDT divisions, such as planning, engineering, and maintenance. Since MDT's different divisions have variable and non-overlapping business requirements for the same transportation data (for example, the Linear Referencing System), it has sometimes been challenging for the ISD to develop cost-effective geospatial applications.

VI. NORTH CAROLINA CASE STUDY:
Organizing a Sizeable GIS Team

CONTACT: L.C. SMITH, GIS DIRECTOR, (919) 212-6001
E-MAIL: LCSMITH@DOT.STATE.NC.US

Background

The initial motivation for creating a GIS program at the North Carolina Department of Transportation (NCDOT) was to address a need for producing planning maps cost-effectively. For this reason, NCDOT's GIS activities originated in the Department's Transportation Planning Branch, formerly known as the Statewide Planning Branch. Early on, the Branch began an effort to spatially organize a database of roadway characteristics called the Universe file that NCDOT would maintain, and then to link the file to digital maps. As part of this major effort, NCDOT digitized the centerlines of state-maintained roads from manually produced Mylar maps. NCDOT staff then used U.S. Geological Survey (USGS) orthophotography to verify the accuracy of digitized data.

No specific person initiated this effort, but the managers of NCDOT's Statewide Planning Branch and the secretary of transportation were very supportive. In general, broad support for developing the geospatial infrastructure was available within NCDOT before any visible projects or applications emerged.

Today, the activities of NCDOT's GIS Unit have evolved to include the provision of a wide variety of GIS services to help meet the business goals of both NCDOT and its counterpart state agencies, such as the Department of Environment and Natural Resources. A variety of data, maps, tools, and information are available as downloads on the NCDOT Data Distribution Center website www.ncdot.org/it/gis/DataDistribution/.

Business Model for Geospatial Technology Implementation

The GIS Unit within NCDOT has been reorganized several times and currently resides within the Engineering Transportation Systems Branch of NCDOT's Information Technology Division. Within the GIS Unit, there are 56 staff positions distributed across three sections (Figure 6):

- Data Compilation
- Product Development and Distribution
- Technology

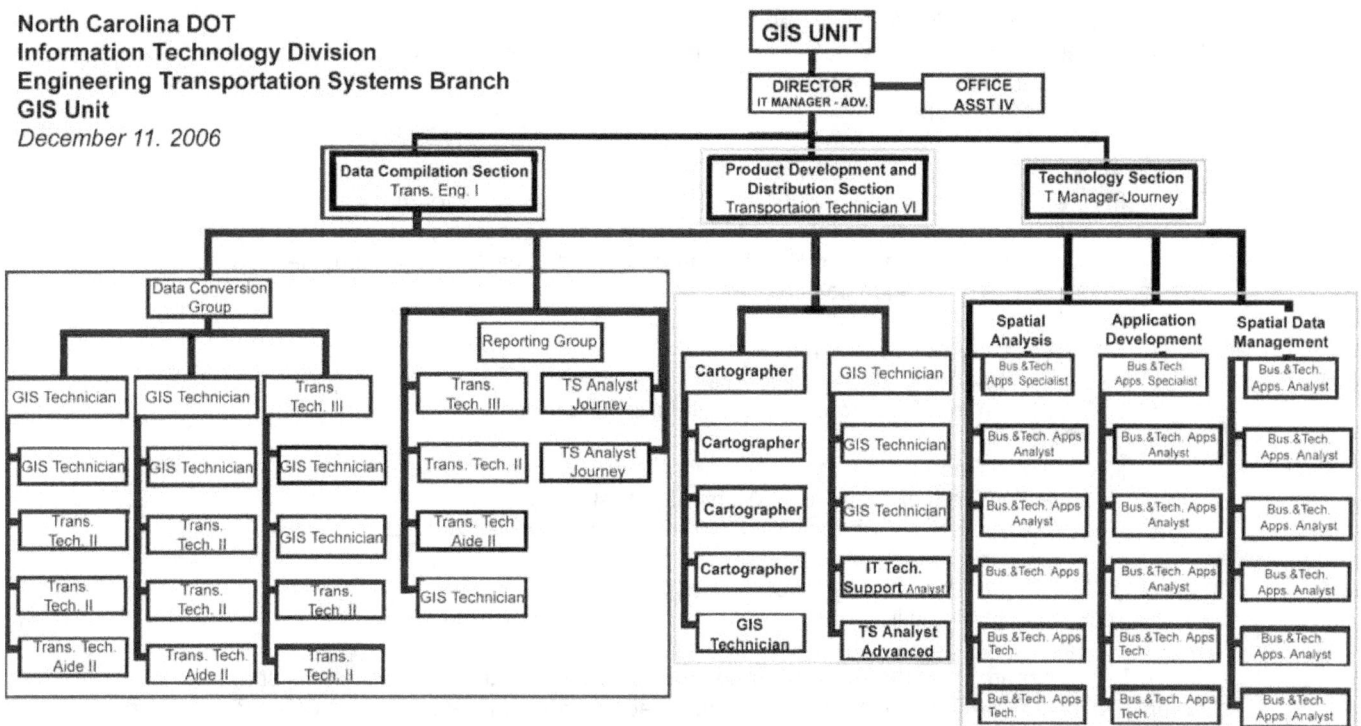

Figure 6: Organizational chart for the Information Technology Division of the North Carolina GIS Unit (adapted from organizational chart received from NCDOT).

NCDOT recognizes that the types of positions involved in maintaining its GIS require information technology professionals, and many positions have IT-oriented job descriptions. Due to the complexity of managing and storing spatial data at NCDOT, even technicians who compile data obtained from engineers and planners to add to the spatial database require IT skills. To express the IT demands of working in the group, the GIS Unit has described itself as "a professional GIS office that relies heavily on information technology to achieve its goals."

NCDOT has been committed to ensuring that current and potential future staff have the skills necessary to work in the GIS Unit. For example, the GIS Unit offers NCDOT staff a one-day "Introduction to ArcGIS (ArcMap/ArcView) 9" class.[12] Externally, the GIS Unit has worked with local universities, such as North Carolina State University, to hire students as part-time and intern staff. NCDOT has also encouraged North Carolina Central University's effort to apply for a grant to educate public school teachers about GIS activities.

Funding
The NCDOT GIS Unit is funded through a combination of state and federal funds (SPR funding). Unit heads or representatives in the IT Division meet every two weeks to review applications for new IT projects, including those submitted by the GIS Unit. These meetings allow knowledge and experience to be shared in the formulation of cost estimates, schedules, and requirements. The GIS Unit then submits proposals for funding from the Department's IT budget to NCDOT's chief information officer for approval. The more expensive IT projects must be reviewed by the Statewide Information Technology Office.[13]

---

[12] For more information on this training opportunity, visit www.ncdot.org/it/gis/GISServices/training.html.
[13] North Carolina Statewide Information Technology Office: www.scio.state.nc.us/default.asp.

NCDOT and the Statewide GIS Community

NCDOT freely shares its spatial data with state and local agencies in North Carolina. With the exception of data layers protected by provisions in state statutes, geospatial information is also freely shared with the public.

This openness is in part facilitated by the existence of the North Carolina Interagency Leadership Team (ILT), an important part of the statewide GIS community. The team, which first convened in 2004, comprises representatives from 10 federal and state agencies involved in transportation planning, economic development, cultural resource preservation and environmental decision-making processes. These agencies are:

- NC Department of Commerce
- NC Department of Cultural Resources
- NC Department of Environment and Natural Resources
- NCDOT
- NC Wildlife Resources Commission
- U.S. Army Corps of Engineers–Wilmington District
- U.S. Department of Commerce–National Marine Fisheries Service
- U.S. Environmental Protection Agency
- U.S. Department of Transportation–FHWA
- U.S. Fish and Wildlife Service

The ILT has prepared a charter of goals and strategies. Its first goal is to develop a shared, comprehensive GIS. The group has recognized that making improvements to a GIS infrastructure shared across agencies is a "critical step toward more effective and efficient transportation planning".[14] NCDOT is active within the ILT, as is the Department of Environment and Natural Resources, whose Center for Geographic Information and Analysis (CGIA) is considered the state's leading agency for GIS.

Another important GIS project at the state level is NC OneMap,[15] an online application for viewing, searching, and downloading GIS data seamlessly across North Carolina. CGIA has been the leading group behind NC OneMap, and NCDOT's GIS Unit has worked very closely with CGIA through data sharing and support. NC OneMap feeds into the USGS National Map[16] and is part of the evolving national spatial data infrastructure.

Work is ongoing to develop a system for assisting small local agencies that do not have the capability to upload their spatial data to a central repository such as NC OneMap. It is expected that such a system would help to expedite the planning process for local projects and the analysis of traffic incidents.

---

[14] Development and Maintenance of a Comprehensive Geographic Information System for North Carolina: www.ncdot.org/programs/environment/development/interagency/ncilt/download/GIS_BusinessCaseSummary.pdf.
[15] NC OneMap website: www.nconemap.com/.
[16] USGS National Map: http://nationalmap.gov/.

VII. OKLAHOMA CASE STUDY:
Pilot Demonstration to Support Enterprise GIS Development

CONTACT: JAY ADAMS, ASST. PLANNING AND RESEARCH DIVISION MANAGER – OKLAHOMA DOT
(405) 521-2175
E-MAIL: jadams@fd9ns01.okladot.state.ok.us

Background

The development and implementation of geospatial technologies at Oklahoma DOT (OKDOT) evolved over many years. Originally, geospatial applications were created to address the specific and individual needs of smaller, discrete projects. However, over time, OKDOT has worked to overcome organizational barriers (such as conceptual gaps in GIS understanding among staff and data silos among divisions) and technological growing pains in order to establish a highly successful enterprise-wide GIS.

OKDOT's enterprise-wide GIS system, the Geographical Resource Intranet Portal (GRIP), allows users to query, view, map, analyze, and report on enterprise transportation data. GRIP provides consistent information quickly, so that more informed decisions can be made about how to improve the quality, safety, and viability of Oklahoma's transportation network. Through the close consideration and quantification of these and other benefits of a robust geospatial program, GIS specialists at ODOT have demonstrated to most Department staff that geospatial technologies can improve their job-performance efficiency as well as the quality of their transportation decisions.

Business Model for Geospatial Technology Implementation

Unlike its counterparts in some state DOT's, OKDOT's Technology Services Division, the division responsible for information technology, does not do much GIS programming. Instead, it manages hands-on hardware tasks, such as server maintenance and workstation support.

GIS activities at OKDOT, including applications development, statewide mapping functions, and historical archives maintenance, are performed within the Planning and Research Division (Figure 7). The Division is also responsible for the development of nearly all transportation GIS data used at OKDOT. In addition, OKDOT manages a tribal boundaries data layer for the 38 federally recognized tribes in Oklahoma and, as mandated in state legislation (Oklahoma Statutes, Title 14, Section 130), a political boundaries layer for the state. Some environmental data layers are provided by other state agencies; for example, the water resources layer is provided by the Oklahoma Water Resources Board.

The Planning and Research Division's GIS activities are supported by FHWA state planning and research (SPR) funds. Annually, the division shapes the initial SPR budget proposal and then submits the plan to the Division's senior management for approval. The budget proposal is then forwarded to FHWA for sign-off.

Due to the Planning and Research Division's responsibility for reporting state highway information to the Highway Performance Monitoring System (HPMS),[17] this organizational arrangement has helped to promote the growth of GIS activities at OKDOT. As described in the section below, OKDOT's enterprise-wide GIS, which the Planning and Research Division now manages, was developed in response to the need for a way to streamline the reporting of required HPMS data.

---

[17] The HPMS is a national-level highway information system that includes data on the extent, condition, performance, use, and operating characteristics of the nation's highways. In general, the HPMS contains administrative and extent-of-system information on all public roads, while information on other characteristics is represented as a mix of universe and sample data for arterial and collector functional systems. For more information, visit www.fhwa.dot.gov/policy/ohpi/hpms/index.htm.

Oklahoma DOT
Planning and Research Division
October 1, 2006

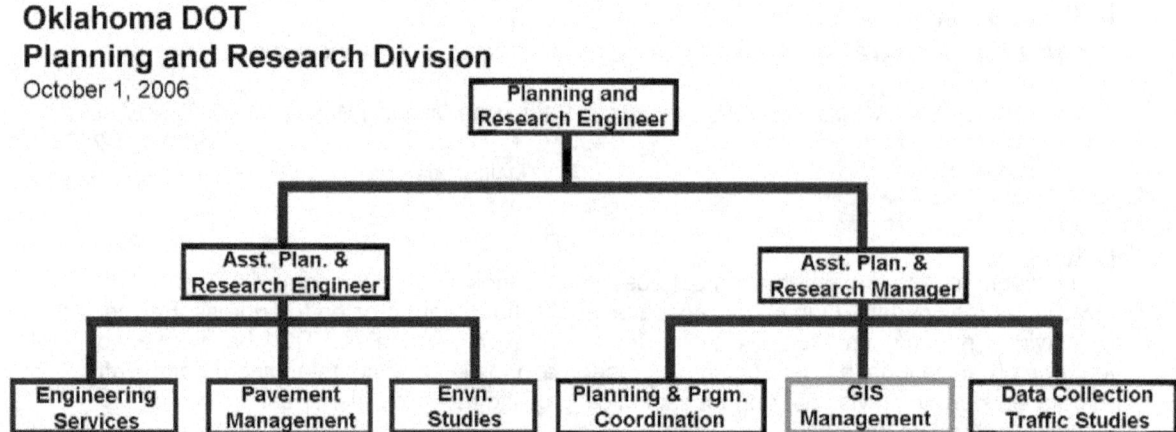

Figure 7: Organizational chart for the Planning and Research Division of the Oklahoma Department of Transportation (adapted from OKDOT's FY2007 State Planning and Research Program, www.okladot.state.ok.us/hqdiv/p-r-div/spr-statements/pdfs/spr2007.pdf).

Enterprise GIS and Related Resource Savings

Each year, state highway agencies are required to file reports with FHWA's HPMS. In order to complete the HPMS reporting requirements, many sources of information on a selection of road-inventory attributes for all of a state's roads must be gathered and coalesced. For this reason, reporting in a timely manner can be a difficult undertaking, potentially straining human capital to problematic limits. In 1996, when the Planning and Research Division's current Assistant Planning and Research Division Manager Jay Adams assumed the state's HPMS submittal duties, the Division began to address this issue.

In 1998, the Division suggested, then developed and deployed an enterprise-wide GIS program for HPMS. The Division viewed GIS as a "great integrator" that could automate the entire HPMS workflow by quickly gathering, managing, and submitting the required data. One year later, OKDOT launched a pilot program to test the system's ability to carry out the HPMS tasks and to demonstrate to senior staff how GIS could manage, monitor, report, maintain, and control the HPMS submittal process. For the pilot, one county with a significant urban and rural road network was selected. The Division did a complete digitization of the network. The GIS was then used to extract data from relevant sources (e.g., aerial photographs, boundary files, road classification data, and survey data) and to complete the HPMS submittal. At the end of the process, it was demonstrated that what previously had taken a team of four to six people several months to complete could now be accomplished by one person in roughly two weeks.[18] In addition to winning a Transportation Planning Award from the American Association of State Highway and Transportation Officials (AASHTO), GIS won over many within the DOT.

Geographical Resource Intranet Portal (GRIP)
The award-winning piloted enterprise GIS evolved into OKDOT's GRIP, an intranet-only portal used to collect and integrate data from more than eight different databases with 32 map themes into a single Web browser for easy access, analysis, and retrieval. Through GRIP, users can access bridge inventory data; bridge inspection reports; pavement management documentation; needs studies; crashes statistics; information on HPMS, at-grade railroad crossings, right-of-ways, and speed zones; and can inventory programs and projects. All staff working within the OKDOT firewall have access to GRIP, including those at the FHWA Oklahoma Division Office, where a special connection to the OKDOT intranet has been established.

---

[18] To view a presentation on OKDOT's GIS-enabled HPMS-submittal process, visit www.gis-t.org/yr2004/gist2004sessions/Presentations/session721.pdf.

It was originally estimated that GRIP would cost approximately $1.5 million to build. Six years later, on release of the third version of GRIP, the estimate ended up being very close; the expense has been between $1.5 and $2 million. OKDOT, however, did not as accurately predict the return on investment for implementing GRIP; the time and cost savings have far exceeded initial expectations. It had been projected that OKDOT would recover its initial GRIP costs within five years. Instead, the costs were recovered within a few months, due to several factors:

- **Information Request Time Savings**—Before GRIP, answering and processing public information requests often took OKDOT staff several days; for example, a request for several different kinds of information would mean requests to multiple divisions. With GRIP, OKDOT staff have been able to access these data instantly through any OKDOT computer with an Internet browser, saving countless work hours–not only for those answering the request but also for people in other divisions whose work would previously have been interrupted because they held the requested data.

- **Emergency Response**—Another area in which GRIP's value has been particularly evident is OKDOT's improved ability to respond to unforeseen transportation problems. For example, on a Sunday in 2002, a barge ran into the Interstate 40 bridge near Webber Falls, causing the bridge to collapse. As part of the response, the state highway patrol called OKDOT and informed it that a detour needed to be established. Since the bridge handled a volume of approximately 20,000 vehicles per day, identifying adequate alternative routes might have been a more daunting challenge without a strong enterprise-wide GIS. However, OKDOT was able to use GRIP to view all bridges in a 50-mile radius of the accident and then review bridge inspection reports. In reading these reports, it became apparent that the bridge offering the shortest alternative route—a bridge that carried 500 cars per day—had a crack and would not be able to support the increased detour volume without repair. With GRIP, OKDOT was immediately able to e-mail directions to the bridge to workers so that the welding necessary for the bridge to handle diverted traffic could be completed.

    Within 2.5 hours, OKDOT had repaired the structural problems and set up the detour. Without GRIP, the effort of manually inspecting the alternative bridges would have taken at least 10 hours. OKDOT estimates that the cost savings generated on that day alone paid for the first two years of the GRIP program.

The Evolution Continues
GRIP has become a model for other states' enterprise GISs,[19] and OKDOT plans on continuing to advance its geospatial activities. In January 2007, the third version of GRIP, which features a graphical user interface based on scalable-vector graphics and allows users to generate reports, was deployed. In efforts to remain "speed-conscious" and to provide state, local, and tribal governments and the public access to some of GRIP's data, OKDOT has worked with a vendor to develop and release GRIPLite,[20] a simplified version of GRIP. GRIPLite allows anyone with a computer and Internet access to view various transportation data layers. While it has been live for approximately four months only, the application has been well received, with roughly 1,500 hits per day.

GRIPLite is especially expected to help the state's tribes to complete the often data-intensive requirements of the Indian Reservation Roads Program, a funding program provided by FHWA's Federal Lands Highway Division. Currently, most tribes in Oklahoma do not have sophisticated geospatial technology or data. Instead of tribal members being forced to go into the field to find

---

[19] Iowa, Kansas, Nebraska, and Delaware are examples of states that have used GRIP as a model for the development of their own enterprise-wide GIS.
[20] To view GRIPLite, visit www.okladot.state.ok.us/grip-lt/index.htm.

and collect data manually, OKDOT can quickly provide the data through GRIPLite. In OKDOT's view, there is no reason to reinvent the data collection, access, and management wheel.

GRIPLite will also likely continue to be a valuable tool for quality control and assurance. With a limited number of OKDOT field staff, it is difficult to go into the field and validate all data that are collected and stored for analysis. Since the public has access to transportation data via GRIPLite, people from far corners of the state are able to pinpoint and report inconsistencies and errors, thereby lessening the validation burden on OKDOT staff.

VIII. COMPARISON OF CASE STUDIES

In this section, case-study states' business models for geospatial technology implementation are compared with regard to five major dimensions: early history, organizational structure, enterprise applications, data development, and funding.

Early history. This category varies from state to state. While some states could attribute at least some of the success of the DOT's geospatial activities to the championing efforts of a specific individual, others indicated that the role of geospatial technologies followed a more natural evolution over a long period of time.

In Oklahoma, a combination of the short- and long-term paths to implementation occurred. There, geospatial applications were initially created to address the specific and individual needs of small, discrete projects. Later, OKDOT, having identified a need to improve the HPMS submittal process, initiated a pilot program to test the ability of a GIS to carry out HPMS tasks. The pilot demonstrated that what had previously taken a team of four to six people several months to complete could be accomplished by one person in roughly two weeks—powerful evidence for executive decision-makers.

Regardless of how geospatial technologies have evolved and been "sold" at state DOTs, most of those interviewed mentioned that, when developing applications, it is critical to understand the business needs the applications are intended to meet. By demonstrating a business case for geospatial technologies, long-term support that can contribute to sustained growth is fostered.

Organizational structure. There was little consistency among state DOTs in this category. The teams responsible for using and managing geospatial technologies at the North Carolina and Georgia DOTs are located within the IT division. At the Arizona and Oklahoma DOTs, GIS units are positioned in planning divisions. Montana DOT organizes its GIS activities across both divisions, while Delaware DOT has GIS staff spread throughout the department.

In DOTs where GIS specialists are employed in more than one division and thus perform different work functions, frequent communication and coordination among divisions occurs. At Montana DOT, for example, a GIS Steering Committee was created to enhance coordination regarding geospatial activities between its Information Services Division and its Rail, Transit and Planning Division. At Delaware DOT, daily discussions among the various divisions' GIS staffs help to ensure a balanced approach to meeting the Department's geospatial business needs.

Geospatial technology use: eEnterprise applications. Two of the six interviewed state DOTs (Delaware DOT and Oklahoma DOT) have implemented an enterprise-wide GIS, while Georgia DOT is the process of building one. These three DOTs have experienced an increase in general GIS knowledge and expertise throughout their entire organizations. These states have also been readily able to demonstrate how geospatial technologies can support and improve transportation decision-making across divisional boundaries. Since enterprise systems reduce the need for single-client software (only a computer with an Internet connection is required) and associated training, long-term cost savings are anticipated. In states with no enterprise-wide system, there is movement toward creating new online mapping tools or enhancing existing ones.

Data development. There are differences in the way that each state DOT first developed the spatial data. Arizona, North Carolina, and Oklahoma DOTs developed their data in-house by digitizing maps that they were already making. At Arizona DOT, many groups within the agency contributed spatial data; information was also gathered from local jurisdictions when possible. NCDOT centralized data creation in its Data and Statistics Bureau. In contrast, Georgia DOT began its use of spatial data with a commercially purchased database; later, it partnered with a major university and used student interns to perform the initial digitization of its own maps.

Funding. Most DOT's indicated that securing funding was key to successfully implementing geospatial technologies. However, most DOTs did not cite budget constraints as limiting the advancement of their geospatial programs.

FHWA's SPR funds finance the geospatial activities of each of the DOTs that were interviewed[21]. Some states may supplement these federal dollars with funding from state-level sources; for example, North Carolina DOT receives funding from its Information Technology Fund. Several DOTs noted that funding is sometimes more readily available for and distributed to planning divisions than it is to IT divisions. In both cases, however, staff must diligently sell the intangible and tangible benefits of a robust GIS to upper management so that funding decisions continue to include provision for geospatial data and applications. To ensure that this happens, Oklahoma DOT has made an effort to explicitly account for the return on investment in geospatial technologies (see case study). Similarly, Montana DOT is including measures in its GIS Strategic Plan for assessing the benefits and costs of GIS applications across divisional boundaries.

---

[21] Funding for Delaware DOT was unspecified.

ACTIVITIES CRITICAL TO SUCCESS AND RECOMMENDATIONS

This section summarizes the key factors for successfully implementing geospatial technologies identified by the case-study state DOTs during the interviews. In instances where there was overlap among state DOTs' comments and suggestions, observations were merged to capture the general sentiment.

Activities key to success that were described include:

- Develop upper-level management support and maintain strong relationships.
- Poll staff and assess business requirements.
- Create a permanent GIS Steering Committee.
- Appoint/designate a permanent GIS coordinator.
- Work to build fast applications.
- Select and define the data architecture for the GIS environment.
- Seek to secure funding for GIS projects from multiple partners, both internally and externally.
- Evaluate available GIS software solutions and document a selected standard.
- Evaluate implemented GIS solutions and document a selected standard.
- Work closely with FHWA.
- Never give up the dream.

Some DOTs also offered recommendations on how FHWA could better support transportation agencies in implementing GIS activities. These recommendations are presented at the end of the section.

Key Success Factors and Recommendations

Develop upper-level management support and maintain strong relationships. Upper management within the entire agency needs to understand and support GIS development—thus, the need for a "constant sell." Sustained support is key to securing the resources necessary to demonstrate steady and visible accomplishments. One way to do this is to continue to track and communicate the cost and time savings generated by using geospatial technologies. Find both formal and informal opportunities to describe to senior managers how geospatial information supports informed decision-making, leading to better decisions. Make an effort to track cost and time savings in order to be equipped with convincing evidence.

Poll staff and assess business requirements. Continually poll geospatial-data end users on staff to gain an understanding of the business needs of various divisions and to determine the features and enhancements to existing applications that are desired. This open communication can help to maintain the trust and support of other divisions within the DOT. As a DOT moves forward with making and strengthening partnerships for obtaining environmental GIS data layers and integrating new features (e.g. video logging, sign/guardrail inventories, truck routing/permitting system) into the GIS, the importance of polling staff about their business needs and their uses of such data will likely endure.

It can also be extremely useful to have an outside person(s) assess the business requirements of an organization. An outside entity can provide an unbiased and balanced evaluation of business needs, better equipping staff to develop geospatial applications.

Create a permanent GIS Steering Committee. A permanent GIS Steering Committee can better coordinate GIS activities within a DOT and across counterpart state agencies. One of the primary functions of the Steering Committee could be to market and facilitate approved GIS Strategic

Plan initiatives both vertically and horizontally within the organization, helping to secure support and funding from division administrators. While other responsibilities could include coordination and possible supervisory tasks (i.e., with a GIS manager), the Committee's primary functions would be to:

- Keep GIS in the forefront of upper management's attention.
- Conduct regular, periodic reviews of and updates to the GIS Strategic Plan schedule and any associated budgets.
- Provide decision-making authority for approving, budgeting, and recommending GIS-related tasks to higher-level management.

The Committee could also formally approve GIS work programs and funding requests, publicize GIS successes, and help to address problems or issues requiring higher-level support and decisions.

Members of such a committee should include mid-level managers from pertinent units who are active GIS stakeholders from a funding and/or implementation standpoint. It is also important to include staff whose units are not yet actively involved in GIS as well as those who may be skeptical about the value of GIS to their unit, as these people often raise important issues or questions that should be considered. A strong leader (chairperson) is necessary to manage members in an appropriate manner.

Appoint/designate a permanent GIS coordinator. Create a permanent GIS coordinator position that has defined responsibilities, including daily operations and long-term planning. This position would best be filled by a relatively nontechnical person who would serve as the single point of contact for GIS and take charge of internal and external coordination for "marketing" and promoting GIS. Part of the GIS staffing plan should be devoted to defining and institutionalizing the responsibilities and functions of this position.

Work to build fast applications. Avoid user frustration by working to ensure that geospatial applications respond quickly to user commands, thereby increasing the chances of subsequent use.

Select and define the data architecture for the GIS environment. It is important that the entire enterprise accept and understand new data architectures when they are introduced. One way to ensure this understanding is to make available an informed facilitator who is knowledgeable about GIS and can work through the process of defining the architectures with stakeholders.

A rule of thumb is to develop user-friendly geospatial applications geared to general business users. Do not overlook senior managers when building applications. A valuable practice is to develop applications that they can use to quickly access and analyze information. Such applications can allow them to see the power of geospatial data firsthand. Upper-level decision-makers can also more easily develop an understanding of the questions that can be asked and answered with GIS, as well as of the benefits that can be demonstrated through the implementation of geospatial technologies.

Seek to secure funding for GIS projects from multiple partners, both internally and externally. Focusing on business needs is the most critical element in developing an effective GIS solution. The expansion of GIS throughout the enterprise is dependent on buy-in from many business units. To develop and deploy more effective GIS-enabled application solutions, partners will likely need to dedicate funding and, possibly, personnel resources.

Funding can be a major obstacle to implementing geospatial technologies, especially within IT divisions. Work with both internal and external counterparts to determine funding needs and to identify how scarce resources can best be allocated.

Evaluate available GIS software solutions and document a selected standard. As part of the software evaluation, an organization must select a standard for the client/server and/or web-based solution that is preferred. This is important for consistency and commonality between delivered software and custom applications that are built in-house or by consultants. The specific version of software should also be identified; thus, the standard will need to be updated as software solutions evolve over time.

Evaluate implemented GIS solutions and document a selected standard. Once a GIS relational database is selected, the specific version of database software to best match with the GIS software must be identified and implemented. This may involve an upgrade of the existing database environment, including applications that use the selected database and servers that house the database environment. If the relational database cannot be aligned with the desired GIS environment due to application limitations or budget constraints, the GIS manager and technical core team can determine the best environment that can be established. It will subsequently be necessary to enforce data standards and to designate a person or group to serve as "enforcer of the standards." Without this function, consistency cannot be maintained and quality cannot be ensured.

Work closely with FHWA. FHWA is often instrumental in providing funding for GIS activities at state DOTs. FHWA is also supportive of workshops where professionals from around the country can come together to share information about standards, ongoing efforts, and cooperation. Some DOTs mentioned that they anticipated opportunities to participate in more such forums in the future.

Never give up the dream. Although making compromises along the way will likely be necessary, it is important to stay committed to the vision of an established and prevalent GIS. While a remarkable GIS can be built around one piece of data, the true power is in being able to compare many sets of data. Sharing a vision for the future with others increases the likelihood of gaining the buy-in and cooperation needed to develop a more robust GIS.

Recommendations for FHWA's Role in Supporting Geospatial Technology Implementation at State DOTs

Support visionary ideas. FHWA can significantly encourage the development of effective geospatial technologies for transportation by supporting new and perhaps untested ideas that may originate at state DOTs.

Support the development of basic, generic, nationwide data standards. To promote implementation of effective business models for geospatial technologies at state DOTs, FHWA could:

- Identify geospatial data needs nationwide.
- Develop generic, minimum data standards at the federal government level.

Such standards could go a long way toward facilitating the integration of geospatial capabilities across applications and data scales at both the federal and state levels. By asking for states' input on their data needs and promoting a shared data standardization effort, more robust geospatial systems might be built. This effort could also later lead to the creation of a Federal Strategic Plan for GIS in Transportation.

A specific opportunity for FHWA to accomplish these goals could be through the Highway Performance Monitoring System (HPMS) 2010 Reassessment. FHWA is advocating that the HPMS 2010 Reassessment be GIS-enabled. In order that some states not view this as an unfunded mandate requiring major business changes, it was recommended that FHWA provide minimum data standards. These standards could improve the quality and timeliness of states' HPMS submittals as well as advance the development and implementation of their geospatial technologies.

FHWA might also help to more clearly define a transportation data model at the national level. It was noted that the NCHRP 20-27 and UNETRANS linear referencing data model has sometimes been difficult to put into practice. Despite the appearance of vendor applications of these data models, research by the Federal Geographic Data Committee (FGDC) and FHWA into transportation data modeling seems to have declined since the late 1990s. Many efficiencies of scale are possible if transportation data models are advanced further at the national level.

APPENDIX A. PRE-INTERVIEW QUESTIONNAIRE

These questions are intended to help collect background information on the implementation of your state's GIS/geospatial program as well as to stage the context of the phone call. No lengthy responses are necessary. We will discuss these and other topics in more depth during the call. Please feel free to send any reports or other existing documents about your GIS program that could supplement the discussion.

1. Where is the GIS program/major activity organizationally located?

2. Who decides on policy for geospatial information in your organization?

3. How are your geospatial applications funded? Was their original development funded differently?

4. From where do you acquire your geospatial data (both the original data and any ongoing updates or additions)?

5. What are some of your notable geospatial applications, and what is their current status?

APPENDIX B. INTERVIEW GUIDE

History/Background/Business Model
1. How did the GIS program at your agency begin?
    i. Was it application-based?
    ii. Who instigated the process? Was it an easy process? Why?
    iii. Who championed the program/process/application or brought it to completion?
        1. How did champion convince others that this was a worthwhile endeavor?
        2. How could executive involvement be characterized? Is there awareness? Support?
    iv. Is GIS work outsourced or done mostly in-house? Do you expect to do outsourcing of GIS services in the future or more in-house GIS work? Why?

2. How many different groups/parties/offices are involved, and how did they become involved? What is the organizational structure?

Data Availability and Use
3. Who administers and/or manages application and/or data? Why? Did you develop your own, buy it or contract for its creation, or work in partnership with anyone?

4. Who currently has access to your geospatial data? All staff, mapping staff only, partnering agencies, the public? (Is it an internal review system/ multi-agency coordination tools or is there a general public version?)

5. In what ways is the GIS program/application(s) helping to make better transportation decisions?

Funding
6. How much has developing your program/applications cost?
    i. How is it funded?
    ii. Who makes funding decisions?
    iii. Does the application save the state money / staff time? Could you estimate how many man-hours have been saved and how much of a financial impact this has been?

7. Is there funding for maintenance? Have staff and funding been allocated for future maintenance?

Obstacles
8. What have been the biggest obstacles to acquiring geospatial information and how did you handle them?

9. What have been some of the obstacles in implementing the program/applications?

Future
10. What has been learned from the setup of your GIS infrastructure? Do you have advice for others undertaking a project/application of this nature?

11. In your opinion, what are the critical success factors for a GIS application and infrastructure?

12. What new projects/activities are planned? Who proposes new projects, and who decides which projects will be pursued?

13. How could FHWA better support agencies in implementing new GIS programs?

www.ingramcontent.com/pod-product-compliance
Lightning Source LLC
Chambersburg PA
CBHW081805170526
45167CB00008B/3327